"One of the most quintessentially Appalachian books I have ever read. *Gay Poems for Red States* is destined to be a cornerstone of the pantheon of books describing what it's like to grow up queer in this country during this time in history. . . . For those having trouble being seen and those having trouble seeing, this book is a blueprint for their shared survival. The love embodied in Carver's voice will set off tambourines in your heart."

—Robert Gipe, author of *Pop: An Illustrated Novel*

"Willie Carver, award-winning teacher and truth-teller, has written a memoir of narrative poems that poignantly explore his experience as a gay man in Appalachia—through food, religion, heartache, and a bone-deep love for the hollers, the hills, and the people. These poems hold your gaze and your ear."

—Crystal Wilkinson, author of *Perfect Black*

"The raw emotion of Willie's words paints a vivid and realistic picture of the life many of us gay folks face each and every day as we strive to transform the minds of our neighbors, families, friends, and communities in the red states we call home. This is a must-read for our community and for any who consider themselves allies. To hear these stories is to know us, to grieve with us, and to boldly advocate for change so that those who come after us might have a life that's just a bit easier than ours."

—Jed Dearybury, coauthor of *The Playful Life: The Power of Play in Our Everyday*

"*Gay Poems for Red States* will be a centerpiece at my equity-driven book shop. Willie's gorgeous personality shines brightly, and the methods he uses to communicate the impact of his intersecting identities are inspiring and insightful. His ingenious use of literary devices both provokes and comforts the reader. He somehow manages to be paradoxically vulnerable and whimsical at the same time, and I can't get enough of his writing. Beautiful. Authentic. Compelling. An incredible work of art."

—Kelly D. Holstine, Minnesota State Teacher of the Year
and owner of WordHaven BookHouse

"Prepare your heart and soul along with your humanity and intellect to feel and be seen by this book. Each line of this incredible text allows the reader to, like his love Josh says, 'find beauty just by expecting it.' Carver reminds us of the gentle yet fighting spirit in us all and why we must keep building a joyous and just world where every student and educator not only belongs but thrives. Oh, how I wish for a world where all students are lucky enough to have an educator like Mr. Carver."

—Juliana Urtubey, 2021 National Teacher of the Year
and White House committee member of the
Advisory Commission on Advancing Educational Equity,
Excellence, and Economic Opportunity for Hispanics

Gay Poems for Red States

Gay Poems
for Red
States

Willie Edward Taylor Carver Jr.
(a gay Appalachian)

 UNIVERSITY PRESS OF KENTUCKY

Scholarly publisher for the Commonwealth, serving Bellarmine University, Berea College, Centre College of Kentucky, Eastern Kentucky University, The Filson Historical Society, Georgetown College, Kentucky Historical Society, Kentucky State University, Morehead State University, Murray State University, Northern Kentucky University, Spalding University, Transylvania University, University of Kentucky, University of Louisville, University of Pikeville, and Western Kentucky University.
All rights reserved.

Editorial and Sales Offices: The University Press of Kentucky
663 South Limestone Street, Lexington, Kentucky 40508-4008
www.kentuckypress.com

The poem "Supermodel (You Better Work)" derives its title from a song performed by RuPaul Charles and features a phrase sung and popularized by the artist. The poem "Clubhouse Character" features several lines of dialogue from the video game *Earthbound*.

Cataloging-in-Publication data available from the Library of Congress

ISBN 978-0-8131-9811-8 (hardcover)
ISBN 978-0-8131-9812-5 (paperback)
ISBN 978-0-8131-9813-2 (pdf)
ISBN 978-0-8131-9814-9 (epub)

ASSOCIATION
of UNIVERSITY
PRESSES

Member of the Association
of University Presses

To my mom and dad, Bessie and Ed, for teaching me
that I was already good enough.

To my husband, Josh, for making their teaching feel real.

The truth will stand when the world's on fire.
    —Appalachian proverb

Contents

Preface

One of my earliest memories of teaching in the rural South happened in a clipped two-minute meeting at Montgomery County High School in Mount Sterling, Kentucky, when an administrator pulled me into an office a few days before the first day of class:

"Just so I understand, you're openly gay?"

"Yes."

"I just want you to understand. In this community, you will be crucified. No one will protect you, including me."

The warning was in some ways a kindness. Speaking uncomfortable truth is never easy and serves only to bring light to darkness. It was stark, ugly evidence of the hatred for queer people that boils just below the surface of otherwise polite places—but it was also an attempt to protect me, as if every Southern queer person isn't already perpetually awaiting crucifixion.

The warning ultimately served as prophecy.

I tried to run away. My husband and I moved to Vermont after that first year so that we could be free to live openly. But, deep inside of me, I was angry because I believed I should be free to exist anywhere in the United States, even in Kentucky, which was my home. I was also angry, even desperate, because I wanted to serve and protect the students of eastern Kentucky.

We returned. I took the same position at the same school. For over a decade, I proudly served students and my community as a French and English teacher at Montgomery County High School. There were setbacks and frustrations (I was a gay man teaching in rural Kentucky), but I made it work because I saw the awesome potential of the children in my room. My rural French students won language competitions against private school students with six years of experience; my high school students outperformed on-campus college students in composition every year; my Kentucky students created an on-campus group, Open Light, that fought for justice and equality and were featured in *Time* magazine; my students taught me that there were no limits to human potential so long as someone could believe in and have hope for them.

It was thanks to my students' work that I was named the 2022 Kentucky Teacher of the Year, an honor among the forty thousand formidable teachers in the state, an honor that ultimately shattered my ability to maintain the necessary hope to see my students soar.

My recognition was swiftly followed by a small but vocal group in my community, led by a single woman, that went to school board meetings and began to make accusations against my LGBTQ-affirming students and student group. They were despicable, baseless accusations that followed the national zeitgeist—grooming, inappropriateness, sexuality—when in reality this was a group of kids teaching themselves history, raising money for mental health awareness, and cleaning parks. The same woman doxed my former students and me in widely shared social media posts showing their faces, pictures of them at work, and more.

The situation grew out of control, and I asked for support. Parents asked for support. Specifically, we asked the superintendent to defend us, to defend the students.

We received none.

There comes a time when anyone working within a problematic, dysfunctional, or toxic system asks themselves if they can continue to resist that system while maintaining dignity and integrity. There comes a time when any minoritized person asks, "Am I safe here?"

Those times came for me in an instant, and a life dreamt up by a gay kid in the hollers of Appalachia, a kid who fought poverty, homophobia, and violence to build his dream, shattered on the spot.

There was no longer a place for me as a teacher.

This collection grew from that shattering. The words, heavy from years of being pushed and hidden far down into my bones so that I might not speak them, so that I might become what I dreamt, refused to stay down any longer.

This collection forced me to ask questions about voice and identity: who was writing—the boy who was afraid to speak to his own teachers or the man who spoke to Congress and to President Biden about the issues children like that boy continue to face? Who was writing—the boy whose only framework was what he had witnessed in his few years within a few square miles in the mountains of eastern Kentucky or the man who has traveled the world and still loves those mountains? Is that boy still here, somewhere, and, if so, how do I protect him?

What I know is that little boy had a right to exist.

What I know is he had a right to dream.

What I know is he had a right to be listened to, and I did everything I could to hear what he had to say exactly as he wanted to say it.

And I want, as best as I can, to share his story.

Minnie Mouse Toy

"Would you like a Hot Wheel or a Barbie, sir?"
The words float like ghosts in front of me
when I speak them, frozen by the winter air
whipping in through the drive-thru window.

"Boys' toy!" Gruff. No *a*. Just *boys'* and *toy*. Two words.
"Okay. We have Hot Wheels and Barbies."
"No wonder you work at McDonald's, you idiot."

Idiot.

I am five again.

My mother's knee-length, interstate-cold
denim coat is a traveling house.
When I stand close enough, I smell
floor cleaner, cigarette smoke, minty gum.
Home.

The bright lights of McDonald's
are a circus of plastic, shining glee;
my tiny heart twists with such rapture
that I feel dizzy and hug the clouds
of home that are her coat.

My mom clears her throat.
"Could I get a Happy Meal with the Minnie Mouse car?"
The words are soft like the quilted lining of her coat,
and each petal of a word builds a flower of *please*.

The cashier hammers a few buttons
and yips our order into a thin microphone,
but then her eyes grab me
and drag me from the coat.
They look me up and down and tug at my shirt.
I pull the coat closer until I am surrounded
by the smoke and gum and cleaner
and can feel the blankets on my bed
piled around me.

But I hear her through the imaginary walls
as she hands the boxed meal to my mother:
"You know you're gonna ruin him?"

The words lodge themselves
into the foundation
of the imaginary home.
It dissolves,
and suddenly
I am just a boy
near a coat
in a bright place with nowhere to hide.

"Thank you."

The flowers are dead. They fall fast to the ground.

My mother carries the cartoon-colored box to the booth,
drops a pack of menthols on the gleaming tabletop,
and gently directs the toy car to the side of the cigarette box
as she lights up a cigarette,
exhales a whispering cobalt storm cloud of mint and worry,
and then fights gravity to pull the edges of her lips into a smile.

"Go ahead and play, bubby. We can eat after mommy smokes."

She tries to ash her cigarette.
I try to play.

The toy car is as heavy as her smile,
and like the smoke,
I know the weight of it is my fault,
and unlike the smoke,
I can't make her feel better.

The plastic is too thick
and the paint on Minnie's pink hairbow
looks like my little baby cousin's cheeks
that change from white to red
while she screams, crying,
and her mom begs her to stop.

I look to my mother's face.

———————————

I pull myself up from the memory.
I am sixteen. I am in a drive-thru,
and the word *idiot* is snowing on me.

"Sir, we have two toys: Barbie and Hot Wheels."

He drives away.
I keep standing.

Supermodel (You Better Work)

When I was in seventh grade, I saw RuPaul donning
    red dress, scarlet gloves, carmine lips
so that she could melodically and rhythmically chant,
"You better work!"
with electromagnetic notes
that compelled me to release the energy of the words with
    every part of my body.

My quick-speaking Appalachian mouth could not contain
the tempo
as it beat drums against the back of my teeth
and stretched the rhythm into my bottom lip.

I'm sure my seventh-grade English teacher
was loudly rolling the library full of eyes,
carefully punctuated
and alphabetically shelved,
in her tenured brain,
when the seven hundredth
"You better work!" flung itself on rainbow-cadenced, musical
    wings
from my mouth
to boomerang across the classroom,
knocking over journals, thrashing against posters, and
    tapping
the musty-paned windows of the classroom
on its quest to freedom.

"You keep singing; let's just hope singing that song is *all you share* with RuPaul."
It was attempted murder by semicolon.

My lips held each other and wrapped around my teeth like a
weighted blanket.

The seven-hundred winged lyrics already swarming the
classroom, however,
buzzing with ionized carols above our heads,
were unmurderable.

United,
they burst through the window and declared themselves free,
and what the teacher couldn't stop
was that I saw it happen
and caught sight of the colors outside.

Goodbye

The last time I said goodbye I didn't know we meant it.
It was probably a Friday.
I'm sorry, but I can't remember.

I bet your shirt hummed into the breeze
with the pine-spice music
that was your cologne, like it always did.

I bet that shirt was blue,
a cerulean flag that I mistakenly pledged to,
not knowing you weren't my country . . .
but I didn't know it was a real goodbye,
so I can't be sure.

Sunsets fade into water,
and memory-kept faces slowly and surely begin to lose shape.
They dry up as time bakes the moisture out of both.

But I know that once
we sat on your bank,
uncomfortable on the rigid and restless creek rocks;
we felt the February water running away from itself across our
    feet,
saw the remaining light stand with icy edges after the fall of
    the sun

as it grasped at colors that slowly turned their backs and
walked away.

And the day was no more.

First Crush

The thing I liked most about Brandon was that he didn't just
    wear a shirt
and he didn't just wear a sweater.
He wore both.
His enthusiastic collars proudly grew out from under his
    sweaters
like cotton walls of radiating emotion:

yellow through blue
green through brown
white through red;
Brandon was the first art I saw
that was able to teach me
just by looking
that when the right things were meant to be together,
beauty was inevitable.

We were both in the fast reader group
(Mrs. Colliver just called us the bluebird group,
but even first graders knew what it meant).
We got to choose who read next
after we finished our sentence
in out-loud group reading,
and once

Brandon chose my name.
Immediately I fell into a pastel dream
in which we would sail to seagull-adorned beaches
and build sandcastles to live in
and have enough money to buy me shirts and sweaters too,
even though
I knew he would lend me his.

Brandon's toast-colored hair was always trimmed neatly,
and his shoes, though white like mine,
were whiter,
like the blank page of a coloring book that I wanted to color in
    all by myself.

One day, my brother, sister, and me had to change schools
because we didn't have electricity in the trailer we lived in.
We never went back.

I still think about Mrs. Colliver's class that I had to leave.
I don't remember where I sat in class
or the number of kids who sat with me.
I don't remember what we were reading in class,
but I do remember the day Brandon chose me to read it,
and on that day, in that moment,
my shoes were as bright as his.

Clean Room

Anytime someone threatened to enter our house,
my mother repeatedly nagged me and my siblings
to clean up our rooms as if, at any moment,
a wandering aunt, nosy uncle, or unsettled church lady
might need to confirm that there were no bowls or dirty socks
    under my bed.

I performed this task with such unique finesse
that she would invite these strangers to bear witness to it.

"Jesus, who ever seen a boy make a bed so neat?"

"You oughtta bring him out to my house after church! Them
    winders are sparkling like they just got saved!"

"You said he *asked* for a vacuum cleaner for Christmas?"

My brother's room, however, was a middle-aged trucker.
Opening his door exposed
an insecure mattress on twitchy cinderblocks
heavy around the waist with dumbbells, bicycle parts,
dirt-covered wires, and other unplanned time capsules.

I could feel myself becoming denser,
lights slamming doors and fleeing peepholes in my brain cells
by my just standing at the threshold.

He wasn't impervious to the weight either,
but no one else seemed to see it pulling him down.

My room was entirely my own,
free to be given any form.
It was slender and agile,
a dancer quick to pose for cameras
and then run
along ley lines that drew light hidden deep in the earth.

It needed to be.

Holes in the wall shrank behind the glory
of framed artwork I made in Mr. Fanning's class.
Broken dresser drawers held themselves up
with all the dignity they could squeeze from a super-glue
    tube.
Cracked windows hid their shame and learned to show off
    their figures
behind long curtains suspended by nails.

No one told me that I could call beauty into being without a
    magic wand,
but living creatures are built with instructions that lie waiting
    to be activated.

Like every creature that knows instinctively
how to protect itself
in a hostile environment,
I, too, found deep in my primordial DNA
what nature and evolution had planted
to make sure I survived.

Found Kitten

I found a winter kitten.
He was trembling and afraid,
his meows like long pulls of a liquid bow across violin strings
    made of psalms.

I was only five or six,
but I already knew enough
to bring him in near the heated floor ducts and offer him milk
    from the fridge.

His fur was gray moss
that chimneyed up into three warm dimensions,
and the soft fabric of his ears whispered to me that he would
    need my protection.

I stacked books like blocks,
some old westerns and new romances,
and made him a home of borrowed words, placing him inside
    to make him safe.

But his meows became distressed,
and he tossed his toylike frame against the books
until they fell into a broken pile of fictional landscapes that he
    fumbled across.

He cried to me
from the other side of the rubble of literature,
and suddenly panic careened through me like molten darts as
    I realized
I didn't know how to care for him.

His eyes lifted,
deepwater basins of worry,
blue-ink printed book stains growing across my hands
until I nervously and repeatedly wiped my palms against my
    jeans.

I didn't know how to protect him or nurture him,
though at that moment it was all I wanted in the world.

Biscuit Girl

"Making biscuits is for girls."
Well, you sure as heck could have fooled me.

Before I even learned to sing the alphabet,
I could make flour, milk, butter, or grease
sing, hum, chant, rhyme, and even shout (if I had baking
    powder).

Butter transforms everything into love between your teeth
    and your tongue.
It's the kind of love that keeps sending you straight home
    after work.

Shortening drifts with you through the atmosphere,
but when you get too high up, you can't smell the weekend fat
    of home.

I can make biscuits drop
like fat, dumpy stalactites willingly jumping
to their deaths
from an ambivalent spatula,
and I can roll out multiple-choice standardized biscuits
that stand waiting
for further instructions,
and I can command them to rise
from a sea of butter until their crusts harden

like carbohydrate continents in a casserole Pangaea.
Why, I can even spoon them and plunge them
into soups one right after another,
so flawlessly
and effortlessly
that someone might call one a dumpling.

As teenagers who worked at McDonald's,
we were sometimes assigned shifts during breakfast on the
    weekends.

They said I couldn't be the biscuit girl
because, well, I wasn't a girl,
but that didn't stop me from carefully observing the process
or from taking over one day when Rachel called in sick.

I was biscuit girl every weekend after that.

Self-Hating Preacher

In my family, there is a preacher
who hated himself when he was a young man.

The mirror-backed insides of his retinas
played rusting memories on loop
that he saw, when he closed his eyes,
just like the rest of us do.

But unlike the rest of us,
his would hold him hostage,
forcing him to watch shadow puppets
engaged in the murky biographical cinema of his life,
dragging him deep into the temporal theater
and tying him to chairs lined with gray matter
while they taped his eyes open
as they forced him to see on repeat
the things he had done.

He tried to break the mirrors
so he wouldn't have to witness himself
and they wouldn't crack,
but with enough time and force and repeated raps,
they pivoted entirely around so that they faced the other
    direction,
leaving him, finally, in the dark of his brain.
Without looking-glass light,

his mind's dark clouds frothing with marionettes
became finally unseeable to him,
but those eye mirrors that used to catch
and cast and reflect his thoughts,
pivoted and flipped to the outside world,
sought once again to project the misery
that had once filled them.

Like lighthouses of self-hatred
they fired enmity from his face,
and their beams singed away the soft mercury lining from the
    eyes
of any person small or weak enough to get caught in their path
and scorched them until those small mirrors were shattered.

I looked him in the face.
And before I could write in full sentences,
I was unable to see myself.

Those glass-beamed threats of gay-burning, sissy-beating
    hellfire
scraped out the soft space behind my eyes,
charring it and broiling its glass into crumbled, black,
    bituminous drips,
letting liturgical coal miners deep into my brain,
where they excavated a rich seam of self
that they desperately hoped to exploit.

The problem with digging too deep or wide into anything
is that it becomes harder to control the dig.
(My papaw taught me that, and he was a union miner.)
So before anyone could have guessed,

they had simply dug too much space,
produced too much fresh-charred soil,
and, as nature would have it, green fields, new saplings, and
    mumbling creeks
called themselves into being from the freshly destroyed dirt,
and in the space between the me
that I was never allowed to see
and the hole he tried to burn,
God hovered and said,
"Let the earth bring forth grass, the herb yielding seed,
and the fruit tree yielding fruit after his kind."
And he (and eventually I) saw that it was good.

Creek

Our trailer perched itself,
proud and ancestral, in a sunny and grass-eaten valley
    bottom.
On its muddy-britches haunches, it stared at the creek
that flattened it out of the holler.

It was a trailer that rolled its cigarettes
with the smell of window air conditioner and hog bacon—
mouth-deep dirt grit and graveled with hard work,
hog bacon was the kind
we killed ourselves.

I killed myself
to leave the holler
and bought pink store pork in smile-scented supermarkets.
But everyone looked at me and could see
the dried mud clinging hard to the bottoms of my shoes.

It asked me if I knew about Jesus.
They couldn't help but stare
or look around or through me
since everyone knows that mud doesn't talk,
and if it ever did, it wouldn't talk about Jesus.

Before such nonbelievers,
I became the valley bottom and my holler,

and the creek swelled within me,
bursting over the banks and spewing out
mud and muck and the mundane and marvelous.

And garbage.
It floated out of me until water,
once brown and muddy,
ran clean and pure and declared unto me
before God and man and animal:
You are the eighth day. You are a creek.

I am always three years old.
Clouds are singing with tambourines.
I'm flat in the mud,
hissing hose still robbing from the well,
stirring up pine straw, gravel, sunlight, and grass.
The water is cool and mossy tin,
but the mud, the earth are love-you warm,
and they both whisper opening flower secrets through the
    thick sheets of trees.

I squish my toes in the mud; put my cheek against
the strong and loving chest of the ground.
No before, no after,
just clouds and blue and brown
and now and warm and being where I am.

I wrap my arms around the earth
and squeeze the weeds,
an embrace that makes the mountains squall in tongues.

I am a creek.
I am dangerous.

I flood.
I keep on going, probably till the ocean,
and I start at the head of a holler.

Cornmeal-and-Water Pancakes

My older brother never seemed to notice things
unless he was pointing a gun at them.
He could hit a pop can
from all the way across the yard
even if the cold was making our fingertips tingle
and the sun was barking into our eyes from above the hill line
and cartoons were on inside the trailer.

I could never make any shot
because there were four-leaf clovers and sparkling zebra rocks
telling wild stories to each other at the rusty feet of the
    railroad tracks.
Who could pay attention to a pop can or a BB gun
with all that beautiful racket?

My mother always paid attention to us.
She told us to come in out of the cold for breakfast,
but her real reason was my sister had just woke up,
and she didn't want her to want to shoot any kind of guns
since she was too little to spell three-count words,
and she still looked out the window
when the Easter bunny was out hiding eggs.
She was also so small
that she squeaked when she said,
"I wish we could have pancakes,"
and a warmer world of imaginary pancakes

rose from behind her eyes, a balm to our cold-numbed faces
that etched a rune into my mother's heart.

"Well, we ain't got pancake mix, butter, flour, eggs, or syrup,
but hillbillies don't even need all that stuff.
Let's make them extra special this morning."

The sunshine stretching through the polyester lace curtains
yawned its buttery warmth across the barren kitchen
in what was surely a magic spell
to make us remember the moment.
Mom lay only the paper cornmeal and sugar sacks from the
    cabinet
firmly on the countertop and told us
we could make pancakes with just two ingredients.
Using the oldest type of enchantments,
she loved the cornmeal and water
with her hands until
it agreed to stay together
as she spread it like a blanket
across the unoiled skillet.
Once, twice, thrice
the fine-ground corn batter
agreed against all laws of physics
to softly brown and turn over in the dry heat.

She boiled water from the tap,
and when steam began
to sing wispy charms as it escaped the water
and release itself into the sunshine,
she held up the bag of sugar like a foundling,
and the crystal powder drizzled out in swirls of cotton sand

that thickened into splashing amber sorghum under her
    wizardry.

Plate clank, steam hum, fork clink, syrup trickle, and syrup
    seep.
Me, my brother, and my sister devoured the corn-
    meal-and-water pancakes,
the corn-grain tufts wearing mud puddles of sweetness,
until, bellies full, we all went back outside to play.

I was scratching a make-believe city scene into the dirt
when my brother broke in to get my attention.
"Hey," he said, kicking a rock across the pretend street
and nearly hitting the invisible school I had imagined there,
"you ever notice that mom never eats when we do?"

My older brother's walnut eyes were obscured by overgrown
    brown hair
and steadily focused on the toe of his cracked boot,
and I had never realized
how much more than pop cans they could see.

Neckbones

The more I know, the more I know that I know very little.
But I know a few things for sure, and I would bet everything I
    know
that no princess ever ate a neckbone.

But I ate a lot of them at my mamaw and papaw's house.

My mamaw and papaw's old wooden house was elderly before
    I was born,
the porch slouching over into its crooked back in front of the
    door,
the arthritic bones of the ceramic heaters cracking in the cold
    mornings,
the uneven windows denser and heavier at the bottom
because of a life of storms, snow, wind, and crying babies.
(I suppose the same thing happened to my aunts.)

When I spent the night there, I slept on the couch
and would unfold myself from sleep
at the beckon of the preaching wall of warmth that grew
from the heater that my papaw would fill with kerosene
during mystical early morning hours that I had only heard
    about from adults.

My mamaw wore a red bandana on her head
and played Ralph Stanley when she swept the carpet;

with each powerful shove of the broom
dust would swirl in the kerosene-warm front,
dancing in the morning sun that squeezed in through the old
    windows,
and Mamaw would pick me up, still wrapped warm in my
    couch blankets,
and deliver me to the kitchen table
because she said the floor was too cold for my feet.

Morning or evening, biscuits or beans,
everything she made was covered in gravy or sauce
because both surround everything
until it becomes part of something bigger.
Love is enveloping
and everyone knows
that in the mountains
homemade gravy is love.

Neckbones exist deep in that old knowledge.
She always served them in an ancient sage-colored glass bowl
that faded toward the lip like it was just too worn out for
    color,
paleontological proof of decades of grease, heat, steam, and
    soap.

They splashed about in the bowl,
floating on a thin horizon of grease,
pearled, flattened globes of translucent, liquid life
that soaked into the soft white muscles of the half-drowned
    potatoes
bobbing between the fleshy bones.

I don't know why she gave us forks.

Eating neckbones meant abandon,
a complete exorcism of rules and regulation.
You'd have to hold tight to the slippery bones,
then grasp the meat with your teeth,
pulling slowly until you caught hold of the gristle,
and then rip away
grease, juice, gristle, and tater falling onto everything.
Sometimes you'd have to spit out tiny bones if you pulled too
    hard,
and sometimes you'd get a big satisfying bite
that would make you feel like you had vanquished a long-
    known foe.

Eating neckbones and taters is the culinary equivalent
of saying *ain't* and meaning it
as strong as a cuss word.
They used to do altar call,
and long-skirted women with wooden guitars would sing
that I was good enough to talk to God
just as I was.

Covered in grease and bones and potatoes
prepared by someone who carried me to the table
necessarily meant that I was loved exactly as I was
and would need nothing more than hunger
to take this communion.

Embarrassing

In the mid-nineties,
it was effectively a law
that T-shirts be baggy and extend below our waists as much as
    possible
as if by obscuring our real bodies well enough
we might directly channel the spirit of Kris Kross (you had to
    be there).

In the mid-nineties,
I was a jigsaw piece from an entirely different puzzle box
and, while I was aware that other boys
wanted to shoot things and wear rat tails and chew tobacco
    and play basketball and lift weights
and spit everywhere and hate reading and call everything gay,
I was content if I could jump rope
to "Miss Mary Mack" with the girls and watch *Star Trek* and try
    to invent
things and learn about recycling and make funny noises.

But in the mid-nineties,
I sure liked those baggy shirts.
I felt freer and somewhat unseen,
and at that time of my life, being unseen was the easiest way
to prevent encounters with children, teachers, adults, and,
    well, humans
who found the easy way to remind themselves

just how easily they fit the puzzle
was to remind me just how much
I did not.

I could cloak myself like a Romulan ship in Federation space
and navigate the star-polluted galaxy totally unknown.

In fourth grade, I was waiting for the bus
and also waiting my turn to jump the rope
when my sister asked me
why I was always curling the bottom of my T-shirt
around both of my hands
like I was about to curtsy
because it looked really gay and it was embarrassing.
(I didn't know I did it.)
Luckily the oversized shirt hid
the flushed skin wildfire that rushed from my face to my legs
and obscured the stomping boots in my chest
as I released the fabric as if I had been
holding contaminated waste
and tried to make my obviously seen hands see-through
while running into the burned woods of my mind.

Embarrassment is a weird idea. You can only feel it
if someone else lets you know that you're supposed to.
It requires two people.
The child of shame, it is most certainly alive,
or perhaps it is the distorted ghost of what it killed,
and in that very moment, the empty-parking-lot voice of my
     aunt
echoed out of my frontal cortex so loud that it caused an
     earthquake,

and her antique words from a fire-lit memory bounced off the
    falling sky:
"We're all laughing at you, not with you."

For the next few months,
I would chastise my hands when I found them reaching
for the bottoms of my shirts,
ripping them away as if they were touching the handle of hell
    itself.
In those times of punishment, I realized
that they only reached out to my shirts because they wanted to
    comfort me
when I felt nervous, scared, intimidated, alone, and different.
I had learned
to punish myself for consoling myself
and to view myself
as a hot handle that could cause pain.

Embarrassment is a tactic of war
in which we teach the other
to destroy themselves
while we can say
that our hands
are clean.

Thank You, Jerry Springer

I didn't hear the word *gay* in class.
I didn't hear the word *gay* in books.
I didn't hear the word *gay* in songs.
I didn't hear the word *gay* in kids' shows.
I did hear the word *gay* in church, but only when they talked
    about monsters.

I didn't always feel like a monster, though I accepted that it
    must be true.
(Our church used to pass out cartoon pamphlets,
and in the special one about homosexuals,
an ugly gay man had horns growing from his forehead
and demons slithering up and down his back;
I used to close my eyes and try to feel the invisible horns
and trap the crawling demons tethered to my soul by lying
    down quickly.)

I tried to imagine a future living in cities big enough
to have grocery stores and homes for monsters like me
since even monsters with horns on their souls had to eat and
    sleep,
though I tied those thoughts up in a bag and swallowed them
and once scribbled them in the thick, graphite hieroglyphs of
    a nine-year-old
on a rip of impatiently thin paper
that I tore from the fragile, dried-leaf margins

of our fourth-grade *Weekly Reader,*
quietly casting the hastily scribbled "I'm gay" into a fire in our
    backyard:
the destructive acts and monster-city imaginings only further
    confirming
the evil I'd been told to believe about myself.

My mom worked the late shift at a nursing home,
and on special nights, she would arrive with snacks, chips,
    and pop
from a gas station she passed on her way home from work.

We would settle in on the couches
amid folding hills of blankets
like ethnographers hiding ourselves
from an uncontacted group of pixelated humans;
against the noisy background crunch of Doritos
and fizz escaping pop bottles like chemically dissolved spirits,
the click of the television remote would deliver us to *Jerry
    Springer.*

Jerry Springer was trash TV in the glory days when people
    thought TV was real.

Cheating couples threw chairs,
men married their mothers-in-law,
baby daddies got freed or tied down
(their words, not mine),
and once the KKK even met with a Black preacher.
For a gay mountain kid with a couch's worth of gas station
    snacks,
it was a precious time to get to safely judge other people
in a world in which I was always on trial.

My least favorite and most favorite and exciting and scary
    episodes
that barged out of the screen and left me with a black eye
were the gay ones.

Sometimes a man would leave his sad wife slouched over,
    crying and broken,
declaring his love for another man seated across the stage in a
    folding chair
as they both drowned under the boos from the audience.

Sometimes men dressed up as women and said they now felt
    happier and free
while their wounded families wept and were washed clean
by the *ooohs* and *aaahs*
of the sympathetic audience.

One time a man told his straight best friend he was in love
    with him
while the audience laughed, and his friend got angry,
but he didn't even throw a chair or run away.

In the small, empty space created
by booed men willing to look at each other,
by ridiculed men in dresses using words like *happy* and *free*,
by men with angry friends who at least didn't even hit them or
    run away,

I hoped against all odds
to find some path
to keep being alive.

Library

The first book I checked out at the library
was about Chinese mythology.
(We couldn't check them out to take home until we passed
    primary grades.)
The broken cover was held together by blue tape, and inside
its battered and bandage-wrapped wings,
it concealed silky reproductions of wall-plaster paintings
from the time when Kuafu chased the sun and drank the
    Yellow River.
For years I worried about whether there were fish in it
and prayed the fishermen in frightened bamboo boats
    escaped
before being consumed by the thirsty giant.

One time the librarian gave everyone a free copy
of a book to take home and keep as their own.
It was about a gangly assistant pig-keeper who left his job
assisting pigs in order to save a bauble-wielding princess
to the background music of an enthusiastic tow-headed bard
as he redeemed his name in an enchanted land.
I used to imagine that similar magic to this
still slept under the moss on our hillside
and gathered itself in holy places
in the dry patches of backyard behind our trailer.
In only a few years' time I was
a white girl in the fifties whose anger kept her alive,

a sister-in-law from Brooklyn who just wanted to be seen,
a son of Indigenous Americans proud of his mother's hominy,
a Black woman in Georgia who learned her power from other
    Black women,
a daughter of Chinese immigrants misunderstood by her
    mother.

They sometimes say that books expand you and your mind,
but they made me feel smaller,
like my world beat its shallow boundaries outward with fists,
wanting freedom
until it couldn't stop expanding
at the speed of light in all directions,
and I became a speck of sand on a vast and endless beach
and finally felt the power of the tide.

Hard to Take Seriously

I thought Mr. Weilder was gay.
He wasn't, but you can understand my confusion since he got
    emotional
when we read a poem by Sylvia Plath about her controlling
    father,
always waited moments before responding to our questions
with woolen words soft and sweet around the edges,
and once apologized for using pink and blue highlighters for
    boys and girls,
suggesting the colors were cliché and sexist.
He was a dry and foreign sprite in the threadbare and muddy
    hills of Appalachia.

Of course I loved him
and with all my might wanted him to see me,
to weep over my words,
to worry about the politics of my color choices,
to hear my question and look me in the eyes and wait years
    before answering.

In ninth grade, I joined his speech and drama team.

We met in the double-wide trailer behind the school.
An overworked aunt of a building, it served dozens of
    functions
when the regular school building was too busy,

and despite being neatly put away against the hillside,
it was always warm and unmoved by the depressed November
    fog,
standing quiet by the hill like it was having a work-break
    cigarette in the cold.

We all read the same poem out loud the first day, and after I
    read,
Mr. Weilder told me I had a strong emotional range
(even though every cell, organ, and system in my body
was feeling only the light bursting out in churchsong
as the bonds of all of my atoms burst apart
by the pull of the single emotion of pride).

We settled on an excerpt from a psychological thriller by
    Robert Bloch
that I was to memorize and recite in its entirety.

I recited it.
I licked every word in the story, to know its taste,
so that I could let people know which words were bitter, which
    made honey,
and which held fire quietly burning between consonants.
I wedged the sentences into my uncles' mouths
to see what secrets the punctuation held;
I insisted the dialogue drive off my grandmother's tongue
and took notes on its speed and gear;
I poured the vapored phrases into Mr. Weilder's lungs
and took pictures of each verb as it escaped his airways
to see which ones reflected light.

For months, every Saturday morning,
I performed for my sleepy-eyed mountain classmates and
    caffeinated coach
in the time-faded Polaroid of that wood-paneled trailer
as seriously as if the moth-eaten curtains were Phoenician
    purple drapes
adorning a fully populated, columned Colosseum
and the desks rose from the floor like marbled stands.

I made first place in our local competition.

After quietly helping form the whispering, shadowed back-
    ground blur
of exactly one thousand baseball and football games
fought and conquered by my brother and sister,
I, for once, got to share a cake with my family
provided by and baked with my power to use words.

The spring Kentucky state competition was at a university
on the other end of the state,
and the judges would be professors
with capital letters and punctuation following their names
and who lived in pitch-roofed houses
with sidewalks and mailboxes
like on television.

I learned what *Columbia blue* meant
because we had to wear matching button-up shirts.

The university was large and clean and smelled rich and
    artificial.
Sienna-bricked architecture tread proudly across campus
with diplomas proclaiming script-printed names

like Augenstein, Zacharias, and Pierce Hall,
which weighed a lot
to a boy who knew grown men
named June-Bug and Chigger.

I fought.

I pulled myself out of the photograph blur until others could
    see me,
straightened my Columbia blue button-up shirt that my mom
    had ironed for me,
and strode nervously to the front of the room
to recite the story.

The words flung themselves out of me in a syncopated
    waterfall,
each drop knowing when to slow or stop,
each stream knowing when to join or crash,
each rapid knowing when to bubble or smooth,
summiting at a bustling stream of words that breathed and
    saw and felt.
I was speaking into existence an old friend
as if I had been given an incantation
who could comfort and inspire at the same time.
I had never performed so well.

Mr. Weilder received our scorecards and comments.
He said some words before handing them to us,
but I didn't hear them because I excitedly reached for the card
twenty times in my mind
before he handed it over.

The handwritten words sucked the color from the room
and punched me in the same chest
that had only minutes before been capable of
reciting magic spells with its breath:
"Hard to take seriously with your accent."

Years later I would drink enough alcohol
to feel the room spinning out of control
(in part to forget moments like that one)—
this same harbinger spin flung me about the university
    cafeteria
as if my body were feeling the resultant drag
from the force of thousands of beams of starlight
all leaving my body at once.

Hard to take seriously   *Hard to take seriously*
Hard to take seriously   *Hard to take seriously*
Hard to take seriously   *Hard to take seriously*

The extinguishing would have been complete
if not for the slow coal-ember fire of Mr. Weilder,
who told me that I couldn't listen to the comments
because there was nothing wrong,
and everything right, with the way I spoke.

His words trickled down the side of my face,
thick with coal sludge.

There were two rounds to go.

My ears and mind were cut by the crisp consonants
and iron-clipped vowels of the recitations given by the other
    students,

who no doubt hailed from cities that were large enough to be
    shown on maps.
I quietly swept myself out of the classroom
before anyone could hear me talk.

Sometimes a person will speak truth
that comes to them years before they are able to live it,
a prophecy and testament to the promise and power of words.

In the third and final round, a woman wearing a blazer called
    my name.
I stood at the podium and felt my ancestors reinforce the steel
    of my bones.
"Before I speak, I already don't care what score I get because
    the first judge mocked how I
talked. I don't think she was qualified to judge me."

I promise to that boy standing
to live up to the spell he cast that day.

Clubhouse Character

In one of the video games
that I played as a kid,
there was a character
who hid in a clubhouse
while the main character,
a boy named Ness,
saved the world.

He only said sixteen words
in the entire game,
and you could beat the game
without even reading them.

But if you found the hideout
and pressed A on the controller,
the boy in a hat,
who was built from 290 pixels,
would say these words:
"You're so cool!
I . . . I think I really like you.
Well, you know what I mean."

I pressed A on the controller
every day that I could
so that I could hear
every sweet word

said from one boy
to another
over and over again
in order to have a reason
to save the world.

It's odd to imagine
that 290 pixels
and sixteen words
could lift an actual child
so far into the air.

Food Stamp Holiday Song

People old enough to remember know that food stamps used
    to be stamps,
paper bills with cartoon colors that reminded us
that we weren't using real money
(even though
no one on and no one off
food stamps needed the reminder),
and they separated us into the kinds of people
who used food stamps and who had real money.

The one-dollar stamps were the thick, Arial-font brown of a
    fat deacon's shoes,
and the five-dollar stamps were the color of grape Kool-Aid.
(There was no chance Mom was ever going to let us in
on what secrets of the rainbow were reserved for larger bills.)

There were two rules known to children who could recite the
    commandment
Y'all close that fridge 'cause that's gotta do us till the end of the month!
(kids who edited out the cuss words for their moms when
    performing it
for laughs in front of the kind of company that gets offered
    coffee,
or when they write about it in poems about those moments
    thirty years later):

1. You will never, no matter how good it looks,
   how hungry you are, or what changes may come
   to this ever-shifting universe, purchase hot food.
2. Food stamps don't come in coins.

The first rule was why they put old fried chicken in a fridge at
      the store:
so that food-stamp kids could remember it was the rich kids'
      leftovers
when it was finally cold enough for us to legally buy it.

The second rule was why I smelled clean
when I sat with those hot-fried-chicken rich kids at school;
as my mom declared in the spaces of my brain owned by the
      Housing Authority
while peeping at a distracted God from the corners of her
      eyes,
Well, they can call us poor, but they'll never be able to call us dirty.

She would look at God the way one might look at a husband
      when saying
that they sure loved coming home with the dishes washed: a
      loud, loving hint.
Mom would divide nine one-dollar brown food stamps
      between three children
who had firm orders for what to do
when we arrived at the dollar store on the other side of the
      hill:
"Now make sure you buy only one pack of gum each, and then
      leave,
or else they'll know what you're doing."
The delicate procedure was repeated once daily

over the course of three days.
(And we got to keep the gum and share it with any friends we
    chose!)

The eighty cents of *real money* we each got back from a pack of
    gum,
multiplied by three children,
received during all three days
of the holy first weekend of the month,
would generate enough money
to provide shampoo, conditioner, soap, and toilet paper.

Getting to the store was an easy walk
because worker men cut through the mountain like slicing a
    cake
to build the road that jogged past our housing project.
My brother would walk us there.

Once it was cold enough for me to resent the pack of gum. It
    was only Friday.

A cashier woman with a red Christmas hat,
looking at my pack of gum and waiting siblings looking at the
    floor,
reached down and tousled my hair. She had on glasses:
"How many packs of gum y'all kids plan on buying this
    weekend?
Go ahead and hand them all over to me, and all your bills too."

My barn-worn hen of a brother had seen more winters than us
    and spoke up:
"We ain't allowed to break the rules. We'll get in trouble."

"Hell, kids. I'm on food stamps, too. I got y'uns. Oughtta be
    against the rules for you babies to
be out in this cold. C'mon. Go get all your gum. I ain't
    arguing."

When a grown woman in a Christmas hat cusses while
    smiling at you,
you really don't have a choice but to put your trust in her.
One by one, she separately rang up the nine packs of gum,
and the cash register beeped a holiday song
about three children
who provided for their family
without having to leave the house again that weekend:

Spearmint Gum, 20¢.	*Food stamp: $1.00.*	*Change given: 80¢.*
Peppermint Gum, 20¢.	*Food stamp: $1.00.*	*Change given: 80¢.*
Wintergreen Gum, 20¢.	*Food stamp: $1.00.*	*Change given: 80¢.*
Spearmint Gum, 20¢.	*Food stamp: $1.00.*	*Change given: 80¢.*
Peppermint Gum, 20¢.	*Food stamp: $1.00.*	*Change given: 80¢.*
Wintergreen Gum, 20¢.	*Food stamp: $1.00.*	*Change given: 80¢.*
Spearmint Gum, 20¢.	*Food stamp: $1.00.*	*Change given: 80¢.*
Peppermint Gum, 20¢.	*Food stamp: $1.00.*	*Change given: 80¢.*
Wintergreen Gum, 20¢.	*Food stamp: $1.00.*	*Change given: 80¢.*

The world did indeed
seem to separate us all
into people who used food stamps
and people who did not,
and that evening,
as I trudged home against the icy gusts
making their way past the mountain
in the cut-through that led to our housing project,
I felt lucky to be in the food-stamp group.

Waiting for God

I was excited and nervous to be baptized
because I thought it would make me
brand new, like a toy still tied up and glued to its packaging,
and also keep me from going to hell.

In the three days until my baptism, I still had fifth-grade
    homework,
and on a Thursday evening salted thick with dogwood and
    cool spring air,
my mom joined me. We stretched out on the tired hood of her
    car
under the Gregorian hum of a crackling housing-project-
    parking-lot streetlight
so that I could color in the phases of the moon with a pencil.
She brought out a blanket and even let me sip some weak
    black coffee.

"Do you think God will wait until Sunday before the end of the
    world?
What if he came tonight and I went to hell?"
She brought the cover around my shoulders,
and her frayed and overworked arms
anointed the bargain-bin blanket with the power to embrace me.
She gestured upwards: "The same God that put them stars in
    the sky didn't do it so he could send
you to hell. He holds them up for a reason. He'll wait on you."

The dark sky became an aquarium of sparks and love, and
     every fish had a name.

Those three days stretched into three decades;
despite the baptism, preachers and lawmakers and winners
     and losers
and lovers and haters and neighbors with tongues and arms
     hot like red irons would
over and over again hold my head underwater,
hoping that the metal hiss of steam would mock me as I
     drowned.

But with each plunge under, the darkness of the water would
     part,
and fish made of stardust would lay hands on me and dance in
     the Spirit.

Gay Road Home

Oftentimes,
the road home
will lead to a
place
you've never
been before.

Salt-Free Funeral

I made the mistake
of looking at her casket
instead of the pulpit
as I wondered from the far pew
that crouched over half hidden like a drunk
trying to get his balance
under the back-wall, stained-glass savior
if they had dressed her dead body
in the bismuth-pink bathrobe
that she had worn every day of the last year
to warm her cancerous body.

In the time I was thinking about my mamaw
and the way she lined her pockets with paper towel–wrapped
　　sausage biscuits,
I didn't know that the preacher had seen me
and, before I could say *fear not,*
he surely began to tremble
and saw me as a city that he was charged to destroy.

He screamed about the danger of homosexuals
that would lead the world to hell on the command of demons.
He screamed that we hated God
and our choices were made to mock the divine plan.
He screamed a lot of things

that lifted into the air above my mamaw in her casket, who
    may or may not
have been wearing a salty, sausage biscuit–lined pink robe.

The little preacher didn't know that he couldn't destroy what
    was ordained by God.

I journeyed to the front of the church,
the eyes of family members like arrows flying and falling short
in sharp parabolas that dared not touch me.

I stood in front of the woman
who only days earlier
had sat with me on the front porch and listened to the birds
    sing.
I stood in front of the woman
who would pat my husband on the knee
as he listened to her tell stories of moving to Kentucky.

I stood in front of the woman
whose strength on its lightning path to me parted the angry
    sea
of pharaohs and chariots and preachers and cowards who
    flooded the room.

I stood in front of a woman
whose pink robe had been replaced
with a white blouse they thought appropriate for the best
    funeral home in town.

But I saw the truth
as she climbed out from behind the cheap paint of her funeral
    mural,

commanding that she be seen while lighting up a cigarette
and draping the bismuth-colored robe around her body
like a secondhand Shroud of Turin.

The preacher continued his attack,
like a suit-clad mud puddle railing
in a drying fever against the shining sun.

I said goodbye to my mamaw,
who rolled her eyes at the scene
and slipped back behind the still-wet paint,
and I made my way toward the church kitchen,
where my kind Lot of a husband surely drank coffee
while making small talk with strange angels offering funeral
    sandwiches.

The preacher was still yelling,
desperate to get his ugly colors to stick to me
when the parted waters fell back together,
but no one in the room was able to hear
the violence of the crashing waves.

I didn't turn to salt
because I didn't look back.

Power of *Ain't*

A few teachers tried to tell me that *ain't* ain't a word,
but the truth will stand
when the world's on fire,
as everyone's aunt always says
with raised eyebrows and lowered opinions.

But on the power of *ain't*,
my papaw fought against men in suits
and built unions out of coal dust and hungry babies
when he said that he ain't doing what men in suits
thought was all he was ever going to be worthy of doing.

But on the power of *ain't*,
my mamaw learned the mystical art
of transforming nothing into good cooking,
into messes of beans and taters with ham hocks
that her grown sons would cry out for in prison cells
because there ain't nothing that craves beauty like wanting.

But on the power of *ain't*,
I set fire to everyone who said no
or even dared to try to get in my way,
and I filled my hungry belly with their ashes
and used the glow from their funeral pyres to light a path
to college diplomas written in languages I learned to talk
    better than them.

Ain't nobody can tell me that *ain't* ain't real
'cause the truth is they're afraid of it—
it is a word of negation and power and taking back
a single pocket knife–whittled stroke of breath that can
hit you back with the switch it made you fetch from the tree,
turn you inside out until your justice is unjust,
and straight up shake the table your game is sitting on.

And there ain't nothing y'all fear like hearing the holy truth
pouring out of the mouth of some dumb hillbilly.

Josh

The first time I saw my husband,
he was wearing a purple polo shirt,
only then he was just a smiling man
who walked into the first day
of graduate-school French wearing a purple shirt.

My cells could already see beyond the cotton threads and
    shuffling syllabi
a beginning that would set the stars into perpetual motion,
and I dissolved myself into electrons and protons
and shifted the fault lines of a solid universe
to command him to sit directly in front of me.

He did.

I could feel the back of his head,
hear the crashing wave of his hair against
the precious peach column of his neck,
could feel the infinite reaching in his shoulders and arms
from worlds and centuries beyond his purple collared shirt,
and for the first time in a lifetime of words and movement
and thought and light and darkness,
I realized that I had never before known where I was.
I knew then where I was.

The brain is made of atoms arranged in specific patterns
and composed by DNA laid out in the dried concrete
of heartaches and lovesickness and joys and fears,
in lonely teenage evenings comforted
by the 2:00 a.m. glow of a television set,
in Polaroid crunch proms and linoleum-sheen school dances
and first kisses and crushes and boys and girls
and knowing that none of it was made for you,
yet somehow,
here you are, existing.

What is done can always be undone,
and what is arranged can be rearranged.
Sitting behind an unknown man on the first day of French
    class,
a man who was and would be my husband,
I felt the concrete soften into clay, felt the atoms cantillating
    in fluid harmony,
felt the world break apart and burn and be remade and reborn
in the span of a single Bible verse.

In that moment, I learned
that even the past has yet to be written
because a world and a time
that had always been made for someone else,
in the span of time it took him to take his seat,
were suddenly meant for me.

A Guy Named Casey Who I Had Never Met

When I was in high school, I had a friend who had already
    graduated,
and she and her mother used to talk about a guy named Casey
who was gay and had moved on to live in a bigger city,
and, though he was gay, they only ever said nice things about
    him.

I saw something ugly
scribbled in the broken handwriting of the sort of broken
    person
who writes ugly things on bathroom walls in gas stations,
and it was written about Casey,
who I had never met.

I scrubbed as hard as I could
until his name faded away from a bathroom in a town he had
    fled,
and I sat in my used car and cried
for a guy named Casey
who I had never met.

Twenty years later
I heard a man named Casey introduce himself;

his voice held the round quicksand vowels and smoky tempo
    of the hills,
and though we were three hours away from the blotted name
    in a gas station,
I knew it was him.

I asked if he was from that town
and if he knew that long-graduated friend and her mother,
and Casey said yes, so I told him about how much
his ghost had mattered to me,
since, though gay and a ghost,
he had left an echo of being loved that gave me hope,
and I told him how I erased his name
from a bathroom in a gas station.

He hugged me tight like we were old friends, and we both
    cried,
even though we had never met,
and he asked me if I was okay.
I told him yes.

I'm Sorry, Chris

I was hiding in the counselors' office.
Plastic green ferns were photosynthesizing fluorescent-light-
    bulb murmur
and pointing at the unashamed brochures on self-esteem and
    pregnancy
that kept the other students away.
It was a space hidden
by the refraction of an academic cement-block mirage,
tucked away for ninth-grade sissies
and boys who played Dungeons & Dragons
and who didn't know where else to go at lunch.

One of them said some boy had dropped a brick
through the ceiling and onto your head, Chris,
and that your angry, queer blood cried out
to the Lord in undulant bursts
like the raging howl of engines
passing under the wheels of a rolling coal train
as the medical workers carried you out
to the ambulance.

I'm sorry, Chris, that your courage
was just too big to fit in that country school
and that mine was too small
even to say hello to you
when you flitted by

like someone the Ancient Greeks would have apotheosized,
your smile fuller than your fear,
your lambent body on holy display
like a statue you dared the unwashed to worship.
I mean, you were the only boy
in the history of the high school
sent home because his shorts were too short.

I'm sorry, Chris, that when I got the nerve
to ask you out junior year of college
and we listened to Tori Amos bounce back
off the bare shoulders of the hill—
that I couldn't hear the exhausted wells
drying out in your voice
because even as you stood on the edge of a cliff,
you made others want to live.

I'm sorry, Chris, that whatever you consumed
to soften your memories
prevented you
from ever making new ones,
and I'm sorry that back when you
were still alive and fighting
for boys like me to live,
I had only yet learned to hide.

Under the Pews

Little boys in country churches
can play with Matchbox cars under the pews
because the grown-ups assume
that they're really too little to understand the preaching.

I held onto that Matchbox rule too long,
with my grasping imaginary arms that were pulled until they
      broke,
and until the adults said that I was too old to play cars under
      the pews.

I was always big enough to understand the preaching.

Hellfire would scream throughout the little wooden church,
opening fire from the pulpit.
I worried the words were aimed at me,
so I would drag myself under the seated churchgoers and
      think that if only
I could imagine hard enough that the little cars were real
and that inside of them were little people going to nice little
      homes
and having nice little suppers with nice little friends,
then I could be somewhere else with them
and not get shot.

But my imagination proved weaker than their artillery,
and the broken sieve of my ears couldn't sift out
reminders that my little gay body would soon burn in hell
and be gnashed upon by teeth as I begged for water;
once I put my fingers in my ears and rapidly and noisily
     ground my teeth
in anxious, scuttling bites
as if my teeth were trying to run away against each other
so that I could get between my mind and the spraying bullets,
but I still heard the whole sentence as it
shot holes in the back of the bench:
"They make caskets for children, and you could die and burn
     in hell tonight."

I ground my teeth so violently
and pushed my open palms against my ears with so much fear
that my aunt noticed my reddening face and shook me back
     into their reality
to ask me what I was doing. I panicked, because
being afraid of a sermon was proof I was bad,
and so I quietly whispered, "I'm praying."

She fell without hesitation to her tired knees,
landing on cheap carpet glued to a particleboard floor,
facing the bullet holes, and bringing her head against
the wood that was worn thin by years of women polishing it
and the constant wear from the weight of worries and
     burdens
that fractured men brought into the church
hoping to leave them with God.
Twisted around on herself and facing the pew,
she brought her hands together,
and she began to fervently pray with her nephew.

The only thing I could do
was talk to God with her,
and so I began to pray
with all my might
for the imaginary little people in the little cars
scattered around me under the pew,
that they might have nice little suppers,
that they might find nice little friends,
that they might feel safe in their nice little houses.

Mountain Learning

If you're not
learning the hard way,
then (sorry about it)
you're just memorizing.

Charisma

I learned the word *charisma*
from a teacher who told me I had it
in the first quarter of my high school joint psychology/
    sociology class.
(Never before had a classroom dictionary brought a fourteen-
    year-old such joy!)

I could sow the rows of that classroom
with seeds of laughter that sprouted and bloomed
in the brain-current flare of a well-timed punch line about
    Karl Marx.

I could convince a study partner
that cultural relativism is not that complicated to get
if you can suspend your disbelief long enough to see
that the people in the North
actually believe bagels are better than biscuits.

I could tie a conversation
with thick, careful rope
and heave Hoover's corporatism until it capsized
unanchored onto the high school football field,
and soon we adolescent hillbillies compared coaches to
    communists,
saw Piaget's developmental stages waiting for buses,

turned school handbooks upside down and shook them
until ethnocentrism fell out from its hiding spot near the rules
    section.

I learned that I could forge any new idea
from the old words printed in bold in our textbooks,
and people would like me for it.

Suddenly the space I had hollowed out
from all the time I spent
living alone inside my head
became a room where I could store
a world that I was inventing.

Scientist

Mrs. White told us that we were all scientists
even though we were only in fourth grade,
and since she brought us gifts all the way from New York
when she went there for a conference in September,
just like she said she would,
we knew that she was always telling the truth.

It was lucky that I was a scientist
because I tripped on the glossy ridge of a smiling dinosaur
    fossil
hiding its face just under the velvety onyx peat
all by itself in the field, where woolen cattails gossiped and
    hushed
over the brooding floodplain just beyond our trailer.

I already knew how to use a phone book,
so I slid my finger down the names that began with W
until I landed on Virginia White.
When she picked up, I told her that we had to move fast
since it was large enough to be a dinosaur skull.
"Well, how exciting! Bring it in."

For two days, Mrs. Virginia White
let me clean and brush the grin on the gray, calcified skull.
It stared at me from the dark and dented empty eye sockets
that waited for me to tell my ossified discovery who he was.

We scored posterboard in metric measurements
and photographed him like a scientific centerfold
laid out on an upside-down plastic tablecloth
that a caterpillar-eyebrowed lunch lady was willing to give me,
but only this one time, young man.

She planted our prehistoric Polaroids
into a manila envelope that bore the address
of a professor of science who worked at a university
that was still in Kentucky
but was so far away I didn't know how to get there.
For weeks I learned via rock cycle worksheets while a dinosaur
watched me with one eye, smirking from the classroom
    bookshelf.

Until Mrs. White shared with me a letter
addressed to Mr. Willie Carver, esteemed fourth-grade
    associate.
The scientist bragged that because of the careful cleaning
and pristine cranial polishing and meticulous measuring
(in well-delineated centimeters) of my found specimen,
he could ascertain almost immediately
the identity of a skull
belonging to a
horse.

He included several printed pictures of a horse in skeletal
    form,
its neck surprising me with its serpentine stretch,
its legs angular cylinders that finished flat like walking sticks,
and its head, all too familiar, flat with cavernous eyes
and an otherworldly foothill-curved mandible that smiled
    because

it knew things about you it was not yet willing to tell.

It would have been upsetting, but it's hard to be dejected
    when a scientist
has taken the time to write you a letter and call you his
    associate.

Mrs. White smiled so wide at me
that her mouth pulled her skin tight around her mandible,
creating an orbital path between it and her joy-pinched eyes
around the exact point
where her eyeglasses rested on her nose.
I asked her if she knew all along that it was a horse.

"What I knew all along," she said, "is that you are a scientist."

Promise

Take it from a fat, gay, weird sissy from up the holler:

sometimes you gotta cry
and let the moon pull
the pain-polluted tide out of your body
onto the shores of your face so your oceans can be pure again;

sometimes you gotta cuss,
gotta hurl hot, raging high-voltage divinations into the air
so they can turn tables and set fire to the hills
to clear a path for you to keep going;

sometimes you gotta mourn
and gather together enough time and space to create gravity
that wraps its roots deep and intimately around a moment
so you can be sure of what was real;

so you go ahead and cry, cuss, and mourn,
but keep your head pointed toward the sky
because this moment will not be the end of you.

Ramen Noodles

I used the shiny seasoning sachet
from a ten-cent pack of pork ramen noodles
to season my soup beans because just plain salt wasn't gonna
    do it,
and I was plumb out of meat
and too tired to get to the store.

I was going to throw the dried noodles away
since no one in a right mind has ever eaten an unseasoned
    noodle
(and you'd be arrested if you tried to buy a single seasoning
    packet),
but a hundred little mamaw voices wearing heavy men's work
    boots
looked out the trailer windows from the darkest parts of my
    cells,
hobbled fast to open the swinging gates in my bloodstream,
broke out in diphthongized hollering that was so unexpected
from their tiny weather-eaten frames
that you'd a thought I was planning on breaking into my
    retirement
to buy a ten-year-old used car from a city man.

Every one of them sized me up from beyond the grave,
their eyes narrowing and their eyebrows floating into the sky,

trying to see if there was any threat of storms in the
        atmosphere,
and they warned in melodramatic rocking-chair rosinings,
Well, now, you might wanna save 'em noodles, child,
y'ain't never know when the creek might rise.

I stowed the noodles deep in the cupboard
and earned two college degrees,
watched every rerun of the *Mary Tyler Moore Show*,
lost friends and found salvation,
swam in the sunlight and smelled barbecue painting itself
        across the sky,
read novels that covered themselves up and went to sleep in
        my hair,
sang snap-together songs on the radio that would disappear
        with summer,
and finally took a new teaching job two counties over
so that I could buy a house on a hill in the middle of town
two miles from the nearest body of water.

We had learned how to move smart by that point,
and every box was carefully labeled and stacked
into neat pyramids of new things we had already owned for
        years;
our empty house was downright thirsting for us to open the
        boxes.

Josh was unpacking the box labeled "Kitchen: food: dry"
and gingerly touching and inspecting every sundry item as if
he might just uncover a latent treasure hidden among things
        he already knew
but that were currently napping between the green beans and
        olive oil

the way he always does when he looks at a rapid succession of
    things—
because Josh teaches me that you find beauty just by expecting
    it.

He lifted from the box, held between his thumb and
    forefinger,
a vague and pox-ridden plastic something that I knew enough
    to recognize as
the haunting horcrux of a dying food chunk
in an opened ramen noodle package that had long ago faded,
its factory creases eroded into earthquake slits
that parted to expose a dried-bone, set-perm, noodly object
now crumbling into powder near scuffed, dusty edges
that were caught in a rapidly collapsing Pompeii death
    embrace.

He held it out to inspect it under the dry light of the stove
    range
as if he had found an unknown shoe in our food pantry box;
a dusty beige fog of ancient noodle dust coughed from the
    package,
and he asked, "What do you want me to do with this?"

At that precise moment of 7:03 p.m.,
way down in Knott County, up the first holler on the right past
    the Save-A-Lot
after a perfectly normal rain,
the creek waters decided to spill over and eat up Doug McCoy
    Jr.'s driveway,
doubling the width of the awnry cousin of a creek
and trapping him and his Ford Ranger at home for a week
for no dang good reason other than because it could.

I took the ten-cent, seasoning-less ramen noodle pack from
    Josh,
covered its scarred wounds in a bounty of masking tape,
and placed it in the back of the shelf
behind the sauerkraut and sliced beets.

Bluegrass Moon

A good friend of mine bore the thin red wisps of her
    sliced-onion scars
that sometimes still whelped and whimpered
with ruptured middle-school déjà vus
to a phosphorescent young girl who was harming herself
because my good friend knew
that pain is so frantic as it drowns
that it can't hear a voice on the surface, and so
she chose to sink so that the girl might hear her.

But not all pain comes from our inability to swim.
Sometimes we are held under the water until we can no longer
    breathe.

Any young'un

whose papaw sucked in the second half of a word like *reckon*
like a tree branch that larrups itself in a snipped-breeze
    buzzsaw snap,

whose aunt thought *could* was too strong a word 'cause it was
    threatening to rain,
so she *might could*—
and she strummed the chords of the first word's vowel with
    such finesse

that the single letter *i* buckdanced with every other vowel with such
vertigo-spun velocity that a lesser man mightta thought it was one single sound,
and the following *t* was so intimidated it just sat down and refused to talk,

whose teacher said, *"You saw, not you seen"*
when he was just gonna tell her
'bout how he seen a bobcat out back
and thought she might find it interesting 'cause she likes cats,

well, that kid would know the waterlogged smothering that comes from
other people getting lost on the road between your thinking and your tongue
and the fear that the only way to get others
to listen to your voice
is to destroy it first.

Monday through Friday, I stood in front of kids like that one
whose vowels and vocabulary become endangered species
so that they could go to college,
and we read Plato and Epictetus, Locke and Xunzi, Angelou and Nietzsche,
and eventually, I started to wonder:
What's the point in hearing other voices
if you never hear your own?

And so I whispered into the wind and changed the weather.

The more complex Nietzsche's moral relativism,

the more I would snow out long flurries of Letcher County
      vowels.

We figured out why Maya Angelou's caged bird was still
      singing
under the wide, flat lightning of an angry Floyd County
      woman's *ain't* and *nary.*

And Xunzi's gentle, dried-flower truths
sprang to April life in the head-nodding *might should* of a Pike
      County mamaw

so that those young'uns could hear
that the best ideas that have ever been expressed
are just as strong and beautifully played
in the music of their own accents.

And eventually we might
set above the elements a proud moon covered in hills:
one that they can see from their desks,
one with the power to lift and lower the tide
so that they can shake off the wet and just walk away.

Trombone

Mrs. Turner had a way of looking at you.

Her eyes would widen like soft, swinging doors to a yellow-lit
    home at dusk,
and you'd feel warm enough, and safe enough, to read
    sprawled on the floor
or to share with the whole fifth grade what you thought a
    poem might have meant.

Sometimes a rare and brief moment of uncovered adulthood
    would unfold
when the science teacher would come to the door
and hide her face behind xeroxed copies of worksheets
that bent under the great weight of elementary school drama
to whisper something head-turning and searing about the
    principal,
and Mrs. Turner's eyes would fly straight upward and right off
    her face.
It felt just like something out of a chapter book.

Very rarely, they focused to a point so fine that the sunrise-
    accented moss
of her eyes would shrink, leaving only the far end of a disap-
    pointed telescope,
and she grew ten feet tall in an optical illusion and felt miles
    away,

and even the cussing boys in boots would sit up straight as she
    exhaled.

One day, her eyes followed us from the oatmeal-colored gym
    hallway
as we left her to choose extracurricular activities,
which we were allowed to do for the first time that year,
but since she didn't come with us,
she didn't see me
sign up to play the trombone in band.

I was not very good at it.

I've heard musicians describing their instruments
like new parts of their rhythmic body that they grow so in
    tune with
that they feel their empty connect-the-dot forms when they're
    not playing.

I felt more like a duck
who had been sloppily grafted with a rhino's horn so heavy
    and distended
that I had to restrain it with both arms to keep it from
    dropping
and ripping off my head.

My parents didn't like the greasy eruption of squawks that
died exploding from the awkward horn,
and my little sister swore that my face was so red and swollen
that it itched her and made her sad to look at me,
so I would stand on the wooden front porch and land on
    dying-mule notes
like a nervous teen trying to learn stick shift in the sleet,

as each brassy detonation bounced off the hill in mad,
    choking brays.

Lucky for my holler, the trombone cost eight dollars a week
    with the rent-to-own option,
and eight dollars was beyond what we could scrounge
    together
because both of my parents had lost their jobs
in the unlucky week after I received my new trombone.
So we ignored the yellow-letterheaded warnings
with "PAST DUE" stamped in screeching red letters that
    arrived in the mail,
and I went to school and carried my trombone
that I lugged to band class for an hour on Tuesday and
    Thursday afternoons.

Until the day, of course, when the men in black arrived, their
    coats still buttoned.
They stomped into the back of the classroom and muttered
    with Mrs. Turner,
so adept at muffled conversation that they didn't require
    xeroxed worksheets,
but Mrs. Turner caught my attention by folding her tactful
    eyebrows
into a bird's wings mid-flight and landing them square and
    fast on my face.

I understood, nodded, and looked to the floor as one of the
    men in black
lifted my trombone,
removed my sticky-taped name from the case,
and strode quickly out the door.

A dumb girl raised her hand:
"Why are those men taking Willie's trombone?"

Mrs. Turner answered within a second, artfully distributing
    crayons
in pedagogical sleight of hand,
to shift our gaze away
from the trombone-shaped hole in the back of class:
"His parents paid to have it cleaned professionally."

My left eyebrow arched into a hill ridge.
Her eyes pulled her head to and fro like a pendulum clock
    running out of battery
as she set her fixed-wall gaze discreetly on my nose.

I never had a trombone after that.

Cogitating

The problem with
a fancy word like
cogitating
is that a person living up the holler
might only find a just cause
and the adequate ventilation necessary
to use it maybe
once a year.

I guess this is my time.

Builder

Everyone lined up to hear my dad build stories
because, just as easily as the man could construct and drywall
   a room
with only the sure creativity of his well-versed hands
and the leftover boards and tin left dying and piled up
on the side of the road in the meat-heavy carcass waste of a
   government project,
he could lay a concrete foundation for a memory quick-
   hardened enough to hold
the rumbling violence of its walls,
and to sheetrock over the scuffed details
so that grown men would edge themselves off their seats
and forget to keep their eyes from growing large as they
   listened.

A man of action whose words could fish a dead cackle out of a
   deacon's wife,
who'd say, "Now, I swear, Ed, you're too much, you gonna get
   me in trouble!"
as she held her bending waist like she needed her hands to
   stop the laughter.
I was sure I was nothing like him,
no matter how much I wanted to be.

Once, while shooting a movie-scene memory at the speed of
    weaponfire
at a makeup counter's worth of my sister's friends from high
    school,
who'd wanted to hear about his two tours in the Vietnam War,
he sat down in his chair, the smoke from his pipe like that of a
    freight train
burning tons of deep-mined coal to keep up with the story's
    pace,
both of his legs extending out of carpenter denim shorts and
    crossed at his feet
as he reclined just so to balance out those moments of action,
like the train was slowing just slightly enough to take a steep
    mountain curve,
and he told them that he carried two injured soldiers with
    bold arms
while holding on to a rope extended from a fleeing helicopter
    with only his teeth,
losing both of his legs to the frustrated gunfire of the Viet
    Cong in the process.

Those girls were so firmly seated in the house he had built
    them
from those recollected yellowing filmstrips of horrors and his
    need to create
something better than what was to change the world again
that teenage girl gasps whirred across the room
like multiple drills hitting the stud at first try in harmony
even though they were
all sitting five feet from the visible legs he had used
to get to his chair to tell his tale.

Someday Child

One time, in middle school,
I was watching *Jerry Springer* with my dad;
the sharp and clean air-conditioner coolness of our new
    doublewide
dried the sweat left over from our summer porch-building,
which laminated me in a clinging, icy buzzing,
and though it was quite a rare feeling,
as I sat watching evening television in a shirt still damp from
    work,
I felt very much a man.

Of course it was a special episode.

A gay man from California cried to his father
as his father said, "I can't accept this"
through large, fanned-out hands that covered his cracking
    face as if he
could hide well enough so that the audience could see neither
    of them.

The awkwardness of the moment
ionized the air-conditioned atmosphere of the room and
    polarized the floor,
pulling my head down so that I was suddenly unknowingly
    staring,

my bare feet backing themselves up against the wall of the
   couch
as if they felt they were trying to avoid some obvious visible
   threat.

My dad, like me, drinks coffee every day of the year, all day
   long.

He sipped his coffee and used a long breath to push himself
   firmly
into the hillside of his chair.

"You know, if I ever had a kid who felt comfortable telling me
   something like that, I hope they'd
know that it would be okay with me."

Time and space were pulled out of the room, and two timeless
   beings stood,
one daring the other to choose this moment to set himself free.

The clock stabbed forward, and my thoughts froze solid with
   the instant impact.

"Well if you ever have a kid like that, I hope they do."

Reassurance

It is important to remember,
especially if you're not the same
as everyone else,
that you can be thankful
and want things to be better
at the same time.

Family Dollar

It had been two months
since Josh said he would like to study French verbs with me
    after class,
and the universe suddenly had texture
that I had never met before.

Every atom and every memory and every leaf and every
    irregular French verb
all tied themselves together with white twine of light strung
    everywhere,
and I could see the undulant smoothness of truth and
    meaning
bursting from philosophy, faces, highways, and spoon
    drawers.

In the parking lot of a Family Dollar
that dug itself a spot to sit
in the baked red-pottery soil of north Georgia,
a thunderstorming memory
built years before I knew about red clay
crept up out of the dirt, shaking itself off,
and sent a shadow surge through the lines that cut off the
    lights.

I cried and shook in that parking lot
as if I had never seen that memory before,

as if it had never before broken in through the windows of my
     dreams
or chanted hateful things into my ear when I was trying
to believe myself worthy of love.

But the sudden contrast between what was and what is didn't
     seem possible,
and it was so sharp that it was slicing through the light
in a heat-lightning spasm of rapid cleavings that I couldn't
     predict,
even though we were in the slap center of a Georgia afternoon
in a used Honda Civic in the middle of the parking lot of a
     Family Dollar.

"I'm sorry," I said, worrying that Josh, too, had seen the
     memory,
and that it had also sliced into the light behind his eyes.

His hand appeared with purposeful calm
like red-ink Bible verses,
and he placed it on my shoulder,
and I felt the memory shriek itself out of my body,
leaving empty spaces everywhere it had been.

"We are not here to be perfect for each other.
We are here to heal what was broken by others."

And his words began to fill that empty space.

Orange Drink Product and Beef Jerky

My first day of first grade was in a new school in a real town
big enough to have a Walmart and movie theater,
and the teacher, Mrs. Jordan, asked if anybody needed change
    for break.

Not knowing what break was, and never having money for
    anything,
I assumed myself a perfect candidate to raise my hand.

Mrs. Jordan's heartbreak and sympathy poured out of her face
    onto me
as I sat in my little blue desk stuffed with
large-print addition worksheets and soft-hued stories about
    animals,
but the sympathy caught my face on fire and burned faster
    than I could run
so that I couldn't hide when she gave me fifty cents for a pop
    "just this once."

For ten years of school we had a lapse in the day to purchase
    refreshments
that somebody once told me funded the boys' basketball team,
and until the year I secured a job at McDonald's, I would find
    excuses

to head to the bathroom, check out a book, or suddenly need
    help
understanding an assignment in any other class than the one
    offering break.

When I was nine, my mom had a great idea
that I could take snacks to school and ask the teacher to keep
    them for me,
so on our trip to get groceries at the first of the month
I scoured the store for the perfect choices,
grabbing a paper canister stuffed with beef jerky
and a plastic-wrapped congregation of orange drinks in waxy
    bottles.

I entered Mrs. Turner's class before the bell rang,
proudly shifting both rations from my Power Rangers
    backpack to her desk,
and asked if she might keep them for me until break.

"So many of these other kids choose sugary drinks and potato
    chips, and here you come
with protein and vitamin C. I couldn't be prouder of your
    choice."

The word choice seemed to me to be worth more
than a lifetime worth of daily breaks,
and I sat straighter in my chair the rest of the day.

Take a Seat

I had two first grade teachers
because our first house didn't have electricity or warm water.
When we lived in that house,
the bus dropped me off at the school where Mrs. Jordan
    taught.

The other kids would read, learn to tie shoes, and sing about
    animals
as I closed my eyes so I could be somewhere else
because taking up space in their class froze my hands with guilt,
and if they noticed me they might see
the nightly cold water-hose bucket baths that made me shiver
floating just behind my eyes.

Mrs. Jordan magically arranged the desks into circles
every day while we were gone to lunch;
they looked like pioneer wagons huddling against an outside
    attack.
We would travel around the camp of seats
while music determined a collective tempo
and then

with a brisk movement of her hand toward a hidden cassette
    player,
the music would die in a sudden jerk,
and the kids in the class would throw themselves

into the nearest seat
like they were afraid of the ghost the music left behind,
and I would stand,
the outsider their wagons huddled against,
until I took my place in the one desk always left far from the
    circle,
perched longingly against the door that led outside.

For what it's worth,
Mrs. Jordan tried hard to help me learn to infiltrate the camp.
We practiced the song before the other kids returned
so that I would know the precise moment of its death
and be ready to find a seat.

More than once I considered it.

But I already knew
that these were their seats,
and worse than feeling the divide that sharply came into
    existence
with the loss of music
was the feeling that might haunt me
if I had tried to take what wasn't mine.
I had already learned
that stealing was wrong
and couldn't bear to take from them.

And so, in almost a year of musical chairs,
I never sat down.

My oldest nephews are both in jail,
and to put money on their accounts,
I hear the metallic clicks of a robot voice

say both of their names in alphabetical order
in a standard accent
so that I can know the number the government has given
   them.

Their younger brother is fifteen,
and this year he stood at the door of the state-of-the-art high
   school,
and despite a brand-new outfit
bought by his mamaw for his freshman orientation
could not push himself across the threshold.
He never went in.

The youngest nephews
sometimes look for me
because their own parents
were so addicted to drugs
that they've been hidden for years.

Mrs. Jordan did not get me
to sit during musical chairs,
but I knew I'd have
to take my place
so that they might see me in it.

No amount
of men yelling *fag* from trucks driving by,
of principals saying I'd lose my job for daring to be what men
   yelled from trucks,
of hillbilly jokes about my bare feet,
or exclamations of surprise at my intelligence
because of the softness of my vowels
could hold back what was meant to be

because every drop of water in every single creek in existence
is meant to join the ocean.

Nearly a decade after I was told I couldn't be gay and a teacher,
this year I was named the Kentucky Teacher of the Year.
And as I watched a camera crew
and heard the governor saying my name,
suddenly the music began again,
and a lifetime of empty chairs circled around me.

I drove to my nephews before the music stopped.

We gathered in a circle in the living room
because I was going to be talking on television
about boring educational matters that made them drowsy,
but before they fell asleep,
I made sure that they got to see
me enter the studio and smile at the host.

As the intro music slowed to an end,
I checked to see they were watching
as I took the first and biggest seat
on the set for the panelists
as if it were built for me.

The Truth Will Stand When the World's on Fire

All of our mamaws' comments about ordinary things
could sometimes vibrate entire rooms in prophetic terms:

"Mamaw, it looks like Jimmy's got that car working.
You reckon he's gonna try to get it all the way
to that college in Morehead?"

"Shew, I don't know. *The truth will stand when the world's on fire.*"

It was as if they saw
from behind their black coffee, church-window glasses, and
      giant print dresses
the end of it all and the connection to everything:
how Jimmy's Sunbird making it to fall semester
might just be the stitch
holding Adam to Moses to Jesus to the End of Days.

In the coal-black shadow mornings of the hills,
such things were too ordinary
and too sacred
to question.

Jimmy's car made it to college.
So did mine.

I was too busy teaching commas and essays
to remember prophecy,
too busy not seeing the world in front of me
to catch hold of the King-James-mountain-witch-woman
    stitches
that held together
the space-time
bending and breaking
in the universes between my students' words,
crawling out from under
the graphite smearing on their multiple-choice quizzes
as they fought the brimstone cement bricks of the classroom
for the right to melt down
truth and freedom
so we could finally see that they were the same damned thing.

It was six years before I saw my first student's suicide note
hastily penned in high-pitched wet ink
on the calloused back side of an old bill of coal miner's scrip.

She was a bright, queer, rainbow-edged life squashed into two
    dimensions
in black-and-white worksheet photocopies
for seventeen years;
we saved her life,
but her paper goodbye remained on my desk,
distracting me as the trucks carried coal to refineries to
    convert it into gasoline,
rumbling and fussing down the hill-carved roads that spied
    on the creeks,
their black-lung soot smothering the schoolhouse windows.

I kept teaching commas and essays,
and the space-time began to fall apart.
The classroom began to wave and bend,
colors seeped through the eroding walls and broke out into
    fistfights,
and the universes demanding to exist
in the spaces between the students' sentences
beat hard from inside the paper,
surging across every threshold
until every ear, every eye, every proton spinning in its nucleus
turned to look.

The suicide notes and goodbye letters
had by this point
stacked themselves so high on my desk
that their weight produced coal
and then oil,
and suddenly the old-knowledge prophecy stitching wailed
    itself into view,
rending the classroom into crackling pieces,
tearing away reality and exposing its frayed dimensions.

The children rose up in a whirlwind as former things passed
    away,
and they didn't ask what to do next
because it has always been written,
and the porch-swept voices of mountain women
thundered across the sky like trumpets playing angels' sheet
    music DNA.
One by one, they would stand
at the edge of my desk:
poor kids,
gay kids,

trans kids,
mountain kids,
hungry kids,
abandoned kids,
angry kids,
seen kids,
real human beings existing as they should
as reality withered down
into the quickly dissolving remains of their high school
    classroom.
One by one, they would stand
with stories waiting to be written down,
and they reached out their hands
as I rolled suicide notes and goodbye letters
and tucked them, dried ink flying into the air like living
    shards of glass,
into bottles half full of gasoline.

We lit the notes.
We threw the bottles.
Then we let it burn.

Hills blazed as smoke rushed dizzily toward the heavens.
Cities cowered and fluttered as they turned to ashes.
Governments were eaten alive.
Fleeing schools turned to salt and shattered.
Churches melted right into the creeks—the heat was hungry.

The world was on fire.

As the last brick fell apart
at the impact of the final exploding bottle
stuffed with gasoline-soaked goodbyes,

the waking creek began to rise,
spilling over on its banks.
The clouds fever-sweating above the explosions below
dropped from the firmament ample sheets
of trying to pray the gay away,
of bathroom politics,
of crying onto handwritten letters,
of self-righteous teachers,
and self-hating preachers
and thin cuts and dead words and broken skin and haunted
        bodies
and shame twisting through the sky in heavy tornado rivulets
in their purest liquid form.

The flood was almost instant.

The creeks rose and sang hymns too old to be written down,
and they called out to God from the ground
as they washed away the ruins of the world.

The former things were passed away.

We surveyed the world made new, washed clean, burned pure,
        baptized in hope,
though its fiery embers still crackled in our memories.

And as mamaws have foretold
since they first made biscuits and whispered stories in these
        hills,
there we stood.

Acknowledgments

Thank you to my many teachers who saw a version of myself that didn't exist yet, especially Karen Taylor.

Thank you to the Kentucky Department of Education for generating the time and space for me to accomplish this work.

Thank you to Abby Thomas, Liz Prather, Lori Looney, Riley Stafford, Jessica Riddle, Kelly Holstine, Meg Marquis, Grete Miller, Layne Neeper, Robert Gipe, and Crystal Wilkinson for the encouragement.

Without question, thank you to Josh for your love and belief in me. I have no story without you.

Thank you to Abby Freeland, Brooke Raby, Jackie Wilson, David Cobb, and everyone else at the University Press of Kentucky for taking a chance on me and for caring about the story of a gay Appalachian kid.

Thank you to every one of the teachers in my 2022 State Teacher of the Year cohort, and to Sarah Brown Wessling, for enthusiastically embracing me and cheering me on.

Thank you to Randi Weingarten, the American Federation of Teachers, and KY120 United for knowing exactly when I needed help keeping the faith.

Thank you to Kathleen Driskell at Spalding University's *Good River Review* for sharing "Waiting for God" with your readers.

Thank you to Ruthanne Buck, Eliza Byard, and everyone else at the Campaign for Our Shared Future for your work, your support, and your kindness.

Thank you to Elyse Eidman-Aadahl and the National Writing Project for understanding how important words are when advocacy is grounded in understanding each other, and for your support.

Thank you to Liz Prather and the Root Deep, Grow Tallers at the Hindman Settlement School for sharing "Under the Pews" and for your generosity of spirit.

Thank you to Lucy and Clayton, my cats, who kept me company without judgment as I wrote.

Thank you to my many students. You have inspired me to believe that anything is possible, and I pray often that your stories are kind, loving, strong ones.